T0372189

LET'S FIND INCLINED PLANES

by Wiley Blevins

raintree
a Capstone company — publishers for children

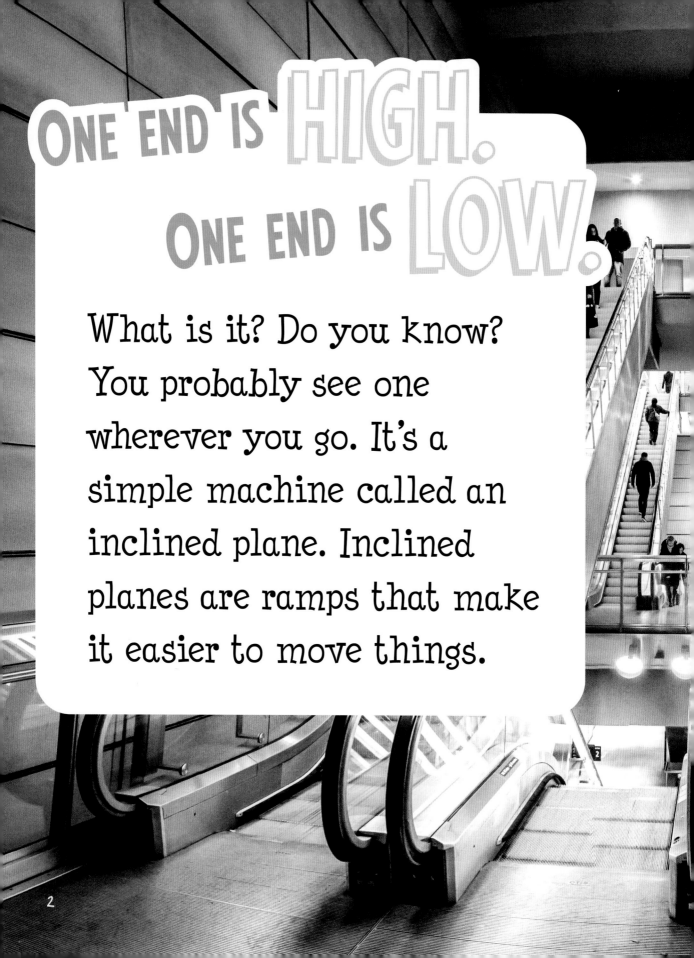

ONE END IS HIGH. ONE END IS LOW.

What is it? Do you know? You probably see one wherever you go. It's a simple machine called an inclined plane. Inclined planes are ramps that make it easier to move things.

How? You don't have to lift things. You don't have to work as hard. Let's find inclined planes!

CLIMB THE LADDER TO THE TOP.

Then whoosh! Slide down, down, down.

4

THIS INCLINED PLANE MOVES YOU TO THE GROUND!

BIG BOXES NEED TO GO IN THE LORRY.

But it's hard to lift them up, up, up. Roll a trolley up the ramp.

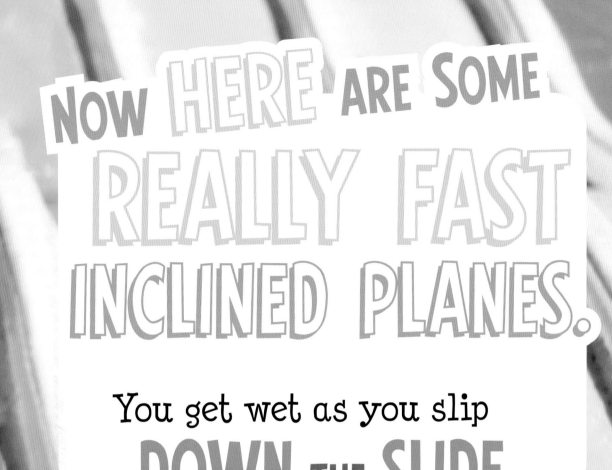

NOW HERE ARE SOME REALLY FAST INCLINED PLANES.

You get wet as you slip DOWN THE SLIDE.

ROLL RIGHT UP.

A pavement ramp is a very helpful inclined plane.

It helps a **WHEELCHAIR** USER GET INSIDE.

TWIST AND TURN!

A road goes up a mountain. How is this road an inclined plane? It's a ramp that starts off low at one end.

THEN IT CURVES AND SWERVES AS IT GETS HIGHER.

RUNG BY RUNG.

A ladder leans against a tree to make a ramp to climb.

GO FROM LOW TO HIGH.

START AT THE BOTTOM.

Step by step, little by little, you get to the **TOP** of this **INCLINED PLANE.**

IT'S TIME TO SHOP!

See all the shops on many floors? There's no need to use stairs here. Step onto an inclined plane!

JUST STAND ON THE ESCALATOR, AND ENJOY THE RIDE!

EVEN A SLICE OF CAKE IS AN INCLINED PLANE!

THAT IS, IF YOU'RE AN ANT!

A BOWLING BALL ROLLS.

Whack! Pins fall down.
But where is the ball?

IT GOES UP A RAMP AND BACK TO THE BOWLER AGAIN.

FANCY HIGH HEELS MAKE A RAMP FOR FEET.

THE HEEL IS HIGH WHILE THE TOES ARE LOW.

CAN YOU SEE THE RAMP AT THE SKATE PARK?

A skater drops in from the top. She speeds up then down.

NOW, WHERE WILL SHE STOP?

HERE'S A FAST RIDE WITH LOTS OF INCLINES.

A roller coaster goes up. A roller coaster goes down.

A ROLLER COASTER ZOOMS ALL AROUND.

stairs

wheelchair ramp

slice of cake

ladder

water slide

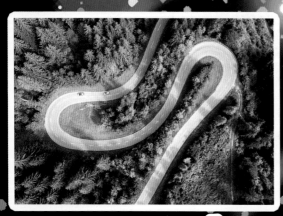

road

ramp

escalator

skateboard ramp

high heel

slide

roller coaster

bowling ball return

Raintree is an imprint of Capstone Global Library Limited, a company incorporated in England and Wales having its registered office at 264 Banbury Road, Oxford, OX2 7DY – Registered company number: 6695582

www.raintree.co.uk
myorders@raintree.co.uk
Copyright © Capstone Global Library Limited 2022

ISBN 978 1 3982 0497 3 (hardback)
ISBN 978 1 3982 0498 0 (paperback)

Edited by Erika Shores
Designed by Kyle Grenz
Media Researcher: Tracy Cummins
Production by Spencer Rosio
Originated by Capstone Global Library Ltd
Printed and bound in India

Image Credits
iStockphoto: andresr, 18–19, CasarsaGuru, 26–27, Charli Bandit, 14–15, Imgorthand, 8–9, kali9, 6–7, vicm, 30 middle; Shutterstock: 3DMAVR, 31 top right, Bill45, 30 top right, BK foto, 30 middle right, elenovsky, 31 middle left, fizkes, 16–17, gmstockstudio, 30 middle left, Gubin Yury, 31 top left, JFunk, 20–21, Kittibowornphatnon, 30 bottom right, Kritsana Laroque, 28–29, Lana Kray, 12–13, Matthew Storer, 30 bottom left, MISS TREECHADA YOKSAN, 4–5, MrVander, Design Element, Oliver Foerstner, 2–3, riopatuca, 10–11, Robert Kneschke, Cover, SabOlga, 31 middle right, Sergey Novikov, 24–25, Syda Productions, 22–23, TerryM, 31 bottom left, Tidarat Kamonmaitreechit, 31 bottom right, yevgeniy11, 30 top left

British Library Cataloguing in Publication Data
A full catalogue record for this book is available from the British Library.

FIND OUT MORE ABOUT SIMPLE MACHINES BY CHECKING OUT THE WHOLE SERIES!

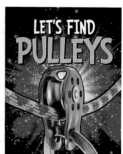